Throw Your Tooth on the Roof

Tooth Traditions from Around the World

Selby B. Beeler

Illustrated by G. Brian Karas

Houghton Mifflin Company

Boston

To Woody, Amanda and Charles,
for their criticism, encouragement,
tech support, laughter, and love
—S.B.B.

For Mary Wong
—G.B.K.

www.houghtonmifflinbooks.com

Library of Congress Cataloging-in-Publication Data

Beeler, Selby B.
Throw your tooth on the roof : tooth traditions from around the
world / Selby B. Beeler ; illustrated by G. Brian Karas.
p. cm.
Summary: Consists of brief statements relating what children
from around the world do with a tooth that has fallen out.
Includes facts about teeth.
RNF ISBN 0-395-89108-6   PAP ISBN 0-618-15238-5
1. Teeth—Folklore. [1. Teeth—Folklore.] I. Karas, G. Brian, ill. II. Title.
GR489.3.B44   1998
398'.353—dc21   97-46042 CIP AC

Manufactured in Malaysia
TWP 20 19 18 17 16 15 14

Has this ever happened to you?
You find a loose tooth in your mouth.
Yikes! You can wiggle it with your finger.
You can push it back and forth with your tongue.
Then one day it falls out.
There you are with your old baby tooth in your hand
and a big hole in your mouth.
It happens to everyone, everywhere, all over the world.
"Look! Look! My tooth fell out! My tooth fell out!"
But what happens next?
What in the world do you do with your tooth?

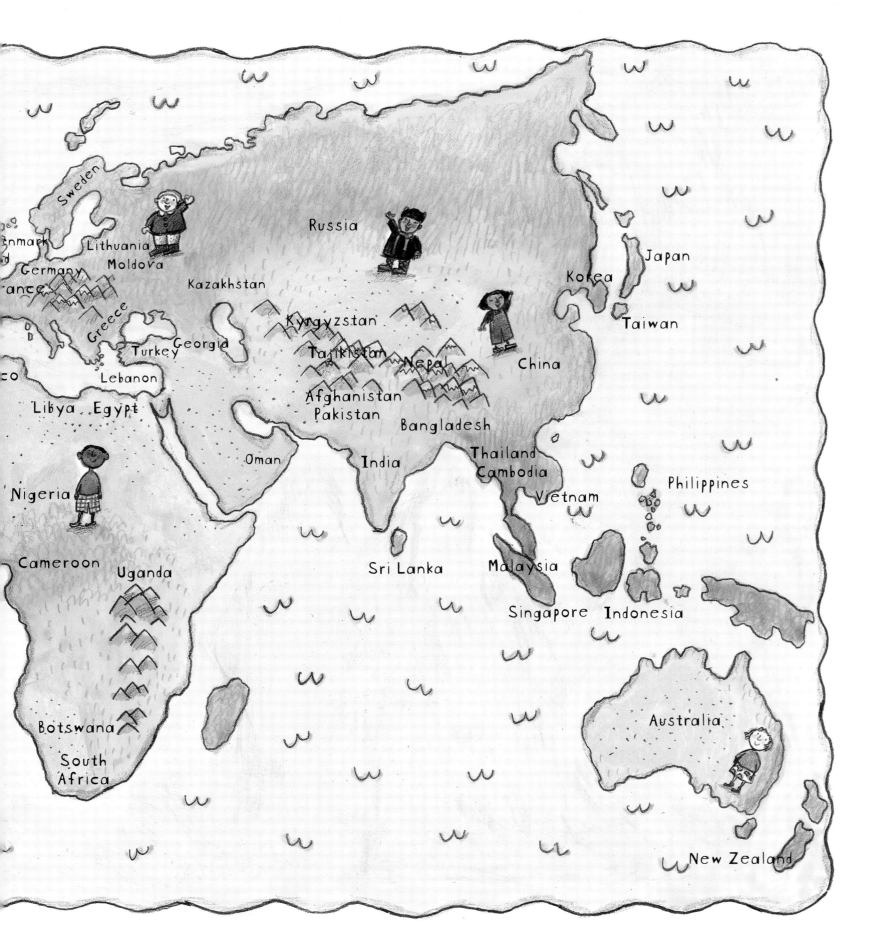

NORTH AMERICA

UNITED STATES

I put my tooth under my pillow. While I'm sound asleep, the Tooth Fairy will come into my room, take my tooth, and leave some money in its place.

CANADA

At night, I put my tooth under my pillow and wait for the Tooth Fairy.

MEXICO

When I go to sleep, I leave my tooth in a box on the bedside table. I hope that El Ratón, the magic mouse, will take my tooth and bring me some money. He leaves more money for a front tooth.

NATIVE AMERICA

YUPIK

My mother wraps my tooth in a food, like meat or bread. Then I feed it to a female dog and say, "Replace this tooth with a better one."

YELLOWKNIFE DÉNÉ

My mother or grandmother takes my tooth and puts it in a tree and then my family dances around it. This makes certain that my new tooth will grow in as straight as a tree.

NAVAJO

My mother saves my tooth until my mouth stops hurting. Then we take my tooth to the southeast, away from our house. We bury the tooth on the east side of a healthy young sagebrush, rabbitbrush, or pinyon tree because we believe that east is the direction associated with childhood.

CENTRAL AMERICA and the CARIBBEAN

COSTA RICA

My mother takes my tooth and has it plated with gold and made into an earring for me to wear.

DOMINICAN REPUBLIC

I throw my tooth on the roof of my house so a mouse can come take it away and bring me a better one. Sometimes I get money when I do this.

EL SALVADOR

I put my tooth under my pillow. My father says that during the night a rabbit will come. It will take my tooth and leave me some money.

GUATEMALA

I put my tooth under my pillow and wait for El Ratón to leave me some money.

HAITI

I throw my tooth on the roof and I say, "Rat, Rat, Rat. I give you a beautiful tooth. Send me back an old tooth." I say the opposite of what I really mean to trick the crafty Rat into giving me what I really want.

JAMAICA

At night, after my tooth falls out, the Rolling Calf comes rattling chains to take me and my tooth away. I put my tooth in a tin can and shake it hard. The noise keeps the Rolling Calf away.

SOUTH AMERICA

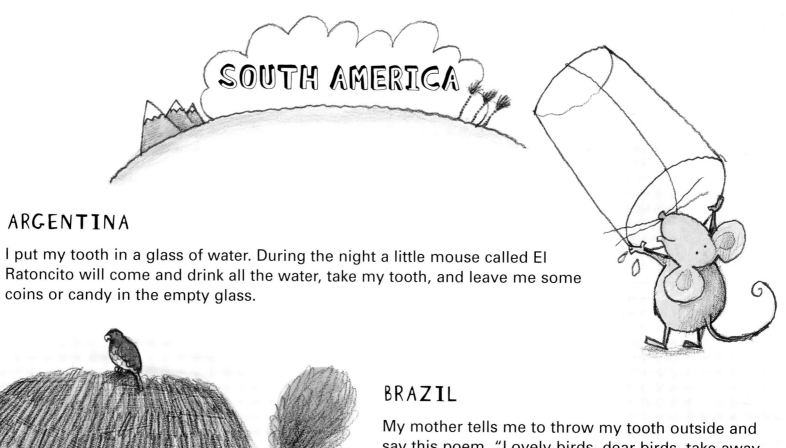

ARGENTINA

I put my tooth in a glass of water. During the night a little mouse called El Ratoncito will come and drink all the water, take my tooth, and leave me some coins or candy in the empty glass.

BRAZIL

My mother tells me to throw my tooth outside and say this poem, "Lovely birds, dear birds, take away this tooth of mine and bring another one to me." The birds only take clean teeth so I must brush my teeth every day.

I also live in Brazil but I throw my tooth out of the window onto the roof and I say, "St. John, St. John, take this rotten tooth and give me a healthy one."

COLOMBIA

I put my tooth under my pillow and wait for a mouse called El Ratón Miguelito to take my tooth and leave money in its place.

VENEZUELA

I put my tooth under my pillow. While I am asleep, a mouse will take the tooth and bring me some coins.

CHILE

I give my tooth to my mother. She will have it made into a charm, set in gold or silver, so I can wear it as a necklace or an earring.

AFRICA—MID and SOUTHERN REGIONS

CAMEROON

I throw my tooth over the roof, shouting, "Take this bad tooth and bring me a new one." Then I hop around my house on one foot and everyone laughs.

MALI

I throw my tooth in the chicken coop. The next day I might find a big fat hen in the coop and my mother will make chicken soup.

BOTSWANA

I throw my tooth on the roof and say, "Mr. Moon, Mr. Moon, please bring me a new tooth."

BENIN

If I lose an upper tooth, I throw it on the roof. If I lose a lower tooth, I dig a hole and bury it in the ground. My grandmother says that if a lizard sees my tooth, a new one will not grow, so I am careful to keep it hidden until it is buried.

NIGERIA

I hold my tooth in my fist with eight stones to make a total of nine (a girl will hold six stones and her tooth to make seven). Next, I close my eyes, say my name out loud, count to the number in my fist, and say, "Oh, I want my tooth back!" Then I throw them and run away. It is very important to run away.

UGANDA

I leave my tooth behind a pot along the path the rats use. The next day my tooth will be gone and I will find money in that spot. Some rats are poorer than others.

SOUTH AFRICA

I leave my tooth in a slipper in my room. Tonight a mouse will come, take my tooth, and leave me a gift. My sister is afraid of mice so she left her slipper outside her door. The mouse left her a present anyway.

EGYPT

I wrap my tooth in some cotton or a tissue and take it outside. I say "Shining sun, shining sun, take this buffalo's tooth and bring me a bride's tooth." Then I throw the tooth high up, at the eye of the sun. (The Arabic word for bride is *aroussa,* which also means a candy or sweet.)

MOROCCO

I put my tooth under my pillow when I go to bed. The next morning I must rise with the sun and throw my tooth toward the sun while I say, "I give you a donkey's tooth and ask you to replace it with a gazelle's tooth." Otherwise, I might get donkey teeth.

LIBYA

I throw my tooth at the sun and say, "Bring me a new tooth." My father tells me that I have a bright smile because my teeth come from the sun.

MAURITANIA

My parents tell me to wrap my tooth in a small piece of cloth and throw it as hard as I can onto the roof of my house. If I get up very early the next morning, I will find a rooster on the roof and I can keep him. If I don't awake early enough, I won't find the rooster.

LEBANON

I throw my tooth into the sea or a field and say, "Oh sun, oh sun, take the mouse's tooth and give me a gold tooth."

OMAN

I face the sun and throw my tooth as far as I can while I say, "Oh mighty sun, take this tooth, play with it, and do not forget to bring it back."

TURKEY

If my parents want me to grow up to graduate from school, they might bury my tooth in the garden of the university. If they hope I will become a doctor, they bury it in the garden of a hospital, or they could bury it in a soccer field so I will be a good soccer player.

EUROPE

GREECE

I throw my tooth on the roof for good luck and make a wish so that my teeth will grow in strong and healthy.

DENMARK

I put my tooth under my pillow at night and wait for the Tooth Fairy called Tand Feen to take my tooth and leave me some money.

ENGLAND

When I go to sleep, I put my tooth under my pillow and wait for the Tooth Fairy to come.

FRANCE

I put my tooth under my pillow. A mouse, La Petite Souris, will come to take it and leave a gift for me.

GERMANY

I don't do anything special with my tooth.

SWEDEN

I put my tooth in a glass of water. In the morning my tooth will be gone and a coin will be in the glass.

SPAIN

I tuck my tooth under my pillow. While I am asleep, the little mouse called Ratoncito Perez will take my tooth and leave me money or candy in return.

EASTERN EUROPE and NORTH and CENTRAL ASIA

GEORGIA

I throw my tooth high up on the roof of my house and I say, "Mouse, mouse, take away my spoiled tooth and send me back a strong healthy one."

KAZAKHSTAN

I drop my tooth under the bathtub and say, "Mouse, mouse, bring me a new tooth, please." We don't have any mice in our apartment but I do it anyway.

KYRGYZSTAN:

I roll my tooth in bread and give it to an animal, preferably to a mouse because they have healthy sharp white teeth that grow quickly. If I feed it to a dog, I might get ugly yellow dog teeth.

MOLDOVA

I throw my tooth on the roof of the house and say "Crow, crow, coming from the mill, I am giving you a milk tooth, now you give me a bone one."

RUSSIA

My mother said to put my tooth in a mouse hole in the ground.

TAJIKISTAN

I sow my teeth in the fields and they grow up to be warriors.

LITHUANIA

I keep my tooth as a keepsake.

AFGHANISTAN

I drop my tooth inside a mouse hole, saying, "Take my dirty old tooth and give me your small clean one instead."

BANGLADESH

I throw my tooth in a mouse or rat hole and hope the mice will give me back strong white teeth like theirs. I usually get a present when I do this.

INDIA

I throw my tooth on the roof and ask the sparrow to bring me a new one.

NEPAL

My mother and father say that if a crow or a bird sees or eats my tooth, a new one won't come in. I bury my tooth in the garden and cover it with soil. Or I might cover the tooth with cow dung or mud and throw it on the roof so it will be hidden.

PAKISTAN

I wrap my tooth in cotton. At sunset I go to the river and throw my tooth in the water. It will bring me good luck. If no river is nearby, I will throw it in a good site, like a garden.

SRI LANKA

I close my eyes and say, "Squirrel, squirrel, take this tooth and give me a new one." Then I throw the tooth on the roof and run into the house without looking.

SOUTHEAST ASIA

MALAYSIA

I bury my tooth because it is a part of my body and needs to be returned to the earth.

CAMBODIA

If I lose a lower tooth, I throw it on the roof. If I lose an upper tooth, I put it under the bed. My parents tell me that the new tooth will grow toward the old one and come in straight.

INDONESIA

I throw my tooth backwards over the roof. My mother says I must throw it very straight so that my new tooth will grow in straight.

PHILIPPINES

I hide my tooth in a special place and make a wish. A year later, if I can still find my tooth, I can make another wish.

SINGAPORE

I throw my lower teeth straight up to the roof so that my new teeth will also grow straight up. I throw my upper teeth straight down to the ground. If I throw them slanted, my new tooth might grow in slanted.

THAILAND

My sisters and brothers tell me to throw my lower tooth on the roof and put my upper tooth under my bed or on the ground.

VIETNAM

I throw my lower tooth on the roof and throw my upper tooth under the bed.

EAST ASIA

CHINA

I put my upper tooth at the foot of my bed and the bottom tooth on the roof. My parents say that it will make my new tooth grow in faster.

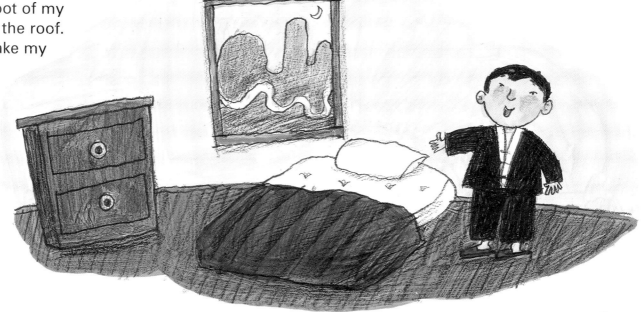

I put my upper tooth on the ground and my lower tooth on the roof.
My new tooth will be pulled in the opposite direction and will grow in quickly.

JAPAN

If I lose an upper tooth, I throw it in the dirt. If I lose a lower tooth, I throw it on the roof. My new tooth will grow toward the old one and will come in straight.

KOREA

I throw my tooth on the roof and say "Blackbird, blackbird, my old tooth I give to you. Bring me a new tooth."

TAIWAN

I throw my tooth on the roof.

AUSTRALIA and NEW ZEALAND

AUSTRALIA

I put my tooth under my pillow and wait for the Tooth Fairy to take my tooth and bring me some money.

ABORIGINAL AUSTRALIANS

My family helps me put my tooth inside the shoot of a pandanus plant so that when the pandanus grows into a tree, my tooth will grow too. There are spirits in the pandanus leaves that will look after me while my tooth is growing.

NEW ZEALAND—MAORI

I put my tooth under my pillow. My parents will collect the tooth and give me a small gift. Then they will throw my tooth into the mighty river, the Waikato. My tribe is named after the river.

Teeth fall out every day, all over the world.

What do you do with yours?

Teeth Are the Same All Over the World

During your lifetime you will have two sets of teeth, baby teeth and adult teeth.

When you are born, all your baby teeth are hidden inside your upper and lower jaws, waiting to come in. These teeth start pushing through the gums when you are about six months old. By the age of three, you will have twenty teeth in your mouth. Baby teeth are also called:

milk teeth—because a baby's main food is milk when these teeth start coming in

deciduous teeth—because you lose these teeth just like deciduous trees lose their leaves

primary teeth—because primary means first and these are your first teeth

By the time you celebrate your sixth birthday, the roots of your baby teeth have begun to dissolve into your gums. Your teeth begin to fall out. This leaves room for your new, larger, permanent teeth to push through. Usually the front teeth fall out and grow back in first. When all your adult teeth come in, you will have thirty-two teeth.

What's in a Tooth?

Crown The part of the tooth you can see. It is covered by enamel.

Tooth enamel The hardest material in your entire body. White shiny enamel protects the crown of the tooth.

Dentin The main part of the tooth beneath the crown and surrounding the root. Dentin is harder than bone but softer than enamel.

Root The root anchors your tooth into the jawbone.

Root canal The cavity inside the dentin that runs through the roots and carries the pulp into the jaw.

Pulp The soft tissue containing the blood vessels and nerves that keep the tooth alive.

Gum The soft pink tissue surrounding teeth.

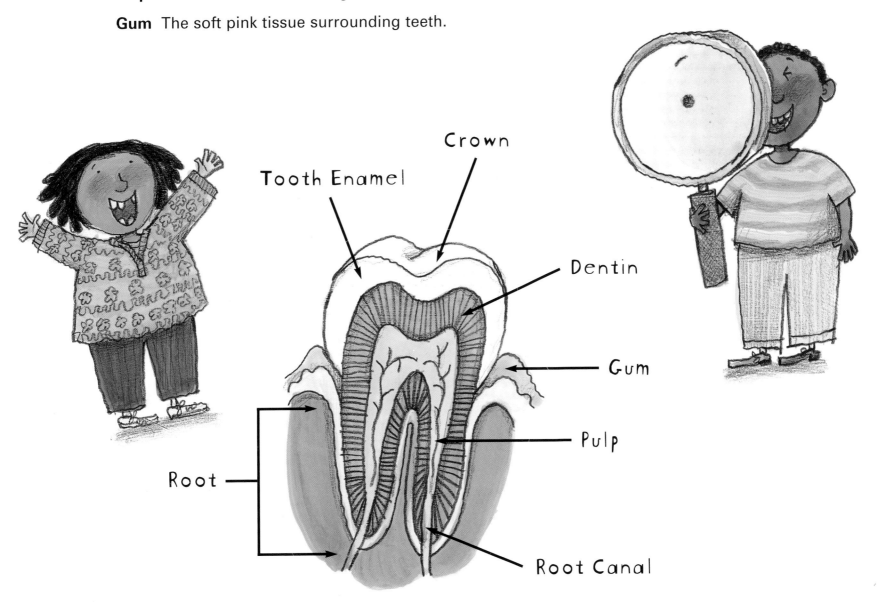

Crown

Tooth Enamel

Dentin

Gum

Pulp

Root

Root Canal

Open Wide

Adults have thirty-two teeth: sixteen in the upper jaw and a matching sixteen in the lower jaw. There are four different kinds of teeth. Each kind of tooth does a special job.

Incisors Eight sharp, knifelike front teeth used for cutting food.

Canines Four pointed teeth used for tearing food. The name is from the Latin word for *dog* because these teeth resemble dogs' fangs.

Premolars Eight teeth, with two cusps each, used for grinding food. Premolars are also called bicuspids (*bi* = two, *cusp* = point—teeth with two points.)

Molars Twelve large, powerful teeth in the back of the mouth, each with four cusps to crush and grind food. The last four molars grow in when you are about twenty years old. They are called wisdom teeth because they come in when you are older and wiser.

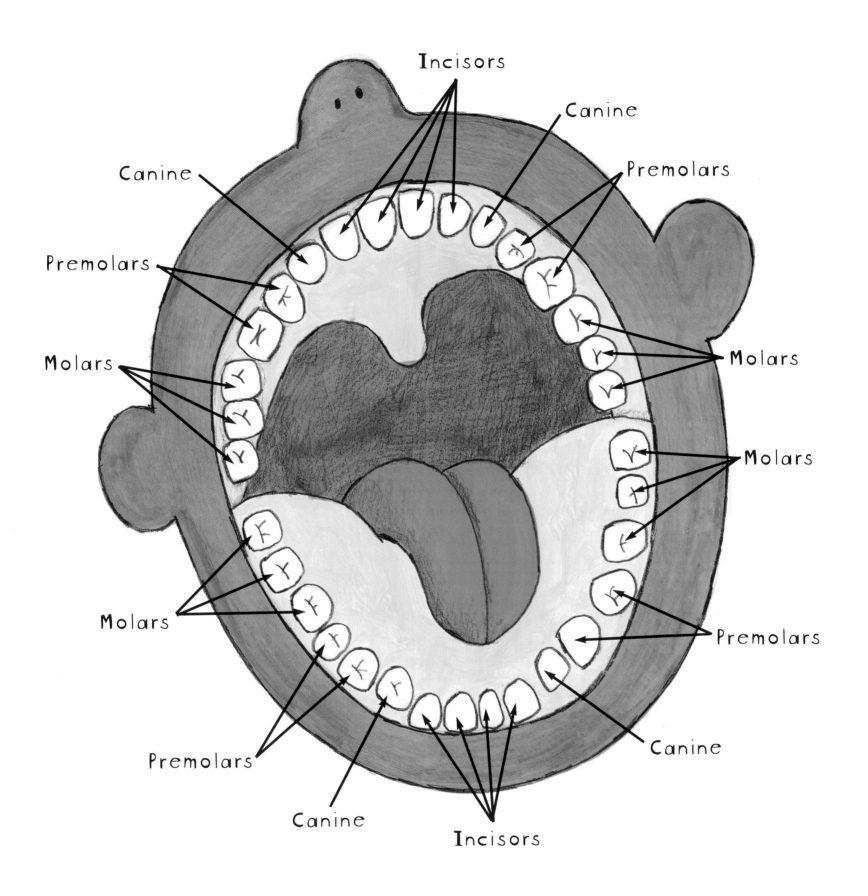

AUTHOR'S NOTE

When I was a child and lost a baby tooth, I put it under my pillow and waited for the Tooth Fairy. When my own children lost their teeth, I taught them to do the same thing. This was the only tooth tradition I knew. One day, as my daughter talked about the Tooth Fairy, a friend from Brazil overheard her and asked, "What's a Tooth Fairy?" Her question surprised me. "If you haven't heard of the Tooth Fairy," I asked my friend, "what did you do when you lost your baby teeth?" Her response sparked my interest in finding out what children all over the world do when they lose their teeth.

I quickly discovered that the best way to learn what people do with their baby teeth is simply to ask them. While collecting customs for this book I stopped people wherever I went. I smiled, introduced myself, and asked them the question I had asked my friend, "What did you do with your baby teeth when you lost them?"

I talked to people on the street, in stores, in taxicabs and airplanes and buses. I visited the embassies of many nations in Washington, D.C., and wrote letters and E-mail to people at universities, cultural centers, and UNICEF offices all over the world. The willingness of strangers to answer my unusual question, whether asked in person or by a note on the Internet, was heartwarming. The friendliness and humor with which they shared their stories made doing this research both fascinating and fun.

In *Throw Your Tooth on the Roof* I have been able to include only a small number of the hundreds and hundreds of tooth traditions to be found around the world. Choosing was not easy. A single country often has many different traditions and a single tradition is often shared by many different countries. I've tried to show both the wide variety and the similarity of tooth customs everywhere.

I wish to send enormous thanks to every person around the globe who so graciously took the time to answer my question. Without your kind and generous help, *Throw Your Tooth on the Roof* would never have been possible.